#SLAY

EAT
SLEEP

circus

EAT, SLEEP, SLAY

Copyright © Summersdale Publishers Ltd, 2018

Text by Hannah Adams

An Hachette UK Company
www.hachette.co.uk

Circus Books, an imprint of Summersdale Publishers Ltd
Part of Octopus Publishing Group Limited
Carmelite House
50 Victoria Embankment
LONDON
EC4Y 0DZ
UK

www.summersdale.com

Printed and bound in China

ISBN: 978-1-78783-314-2

Substantial discounts on bulk quantities of Summersdale books are available to corporations, professional associations and other organizations. For details contact general enquiries: telephone: +44 (0) 1243 771107 or email: enquiries@summersdale.com.

10 9 8 7 6 5 4 3 2 1

TO . . . .

FROM . . . .

ALL WOMEN ARE NATURALLY BADASS.

ALICIA KEYS

BRING YOUR YOUR SLAY GAME

I'M NOT BOSSY. I'M THE BOSS.

BEYONCÉ

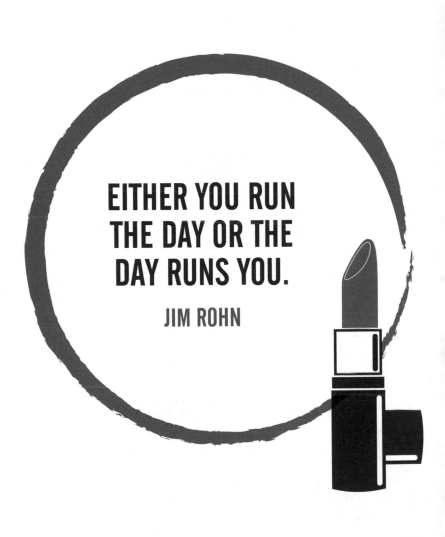

EITHER YOU RUN
THE DAY OR THE
DAY RUNS YOU.

JIM ROHN

Do your squats, eat your vegetables, wear red lipstick, don't let boys be mean to you.

Kendall Jenner

TAKE EVERY CHANCE YOU GET

Stay afraid, but do
it anyway. What's
important is the action.

Carrie Fisher

YOU ARE NEVER TOO OLD
TO SET ANOTHER GOAL OR
TO DREAM A NEW DREAM.

Les Brown

OTHER WOMEN
WHO ARE KILLING IT
SHOULD MOTIVATE
YOU, THRILL YOU,
CHALLENGE YOU
AND INSPIRE YOU.

Taylor Swift

KNOW YOUR WORTH,

then add

Tax

BETTER TO LIVE ONE YEAR AS A TIGER, THAN A HUNDRED AS A SHEEP.

MADONNA

NEVER DOUBT THAT YOU ARE VALUABLE AND POWERFUL AND DESERVING OF EVERY CHANCE AND OPPORTUNITY IN THE WORLD.

Hillary Clinton

DO A LITTLE MORE EACH DAY THAN YOU THINK YOU POSSIBLY CAN.

LOWELL THOMAS

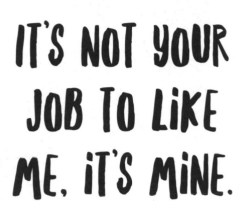

IT'S NOT YOUR
JOB TO LIKE
ME, IT'S MINE.

BYRON KATIE

BEHIND
EVERY
SUCCESSFUL
WOMAN IS
HERSELF

I'M NOT THE NEXT USAIN
BOLT OR MICHAEL PHELPS.
I'M THE FIRST SIMONE BILES.

Simone Biles

SET YOUR GOALS HIGH, AND DON'T STOP TILL YOU GET THERE.

BO JACKSON

FRIENDS WHO SLAY TOGETHER

stay together

IF NOT ME, WHO? IF NOT NOW, WHEN?

EMMA WATSON

KNOW WHAT? B*TCHES GET STUFF DONE.

TINA FEY

ENTHUSIASM MOVES

THE WORLD.

Arthur Balfour

I'm done compromising;
even more so, I'm done
with being compromised.

Mila Kunis

I want to be
remembered as the
girl who stood up.

Malala Yousafzai

GIRL,
YOU
GOT THIS

SOMETIMES YOU GOTTA BE A BEAUTY AND A BEAST.

NICKI MINAJ

IT'S ALWAYS TOO EARLY TO QUIT.

NORMAN VINCENT PEALE

All the marks on
the world mean
nothing compared
to the marks you're
about to make.

Amber Tamblyn

TOO GLAM TO GIVE A DAMN

I'M OVER TRYING TO FIND
THE 'ADORABLE' WAY TO
STATE MY OPINION AND
STILL BE LIKABLE!

Jennifer Lawrence

I LOVE
MY REJECTION
SLIPS. THEY
SHOW ME I TRY.

SYLVIA PLATH

RUN TO THE FIRE; DON'T HIDE FROM IT.

MEG WHITMAN

You have to stand for
what you believe in and
sometimes you have
to stand alone.

Queen Latifah

ALWAYS
WEAR YOUR
INVISIBLE
CROWN

I GOT MY
OWN BACK.

MAYA ANGELOU

WHEN LIFE
SEEMS HARD, THE
COURAGEOUS DO
NOT LIE DOWN AND
ACCEPT DEFEAT;
INSTEAD, THEY
ARE ALL THE MORE
DETERMINED TO
STRUGGLE FOR A
BETTER FUTURE.

Queen Elizabeth II

A girl doesn't
need anyone who
doesn't need her.

Marilyn Monroe

I'VE BEEN THROUGH IT ALL, BABY, I'M MOTHER COURAGE.

ELIZABETH TAYLOR

EMPOWERED WOMEN EMPOWER WOMEN

MY COACH SAID I
RAN LIKE A GIRL.
I SAID IF HE RAN
A LITTLE FASTER
HE COULD TOO.

MIA HAMM

THE BEST WAY TO
MAKE YOUR DREAMS
COME TRUE IS TO
WAKE UP.

PAUL VALÉRY

I DON'T GET BITTER, I JUST GET BETTER.

RIHANNA

BUCKLE UP, AND KNOW
THAT IT'S GOING TO BE A
TREMENDOUS AMOUNT OF
WORK, BUT EMBRACE IT.

Tory Burch

ACTUALLY, I CAN

UNLESS THEY GONNA PAY YOUR BILLS, PAY THEM B*TCHES NO MIND.

RuPaul

I wouldn't do anything,
I wouldn't work anywhere,
if I wasn't interested in
getting to the very top.

Jess Phillips

I'M STRONG,
I'M TOUGH,
I STILL WEAR
MY EYELINER.

LISA LESLIE

BEYONCÉ WASN'T BUILT IN A DAY

I'm not intimidated
by how people
perceive me.

Dolly Parton

THERE IS NO SUBSTITUTE FOR HARD WORK.

THOMAS EDISON

GIRLS GOT BALLS. THEY'RE JUST A LITTLE HIGHER UP.

JOAN JETT

Never grow a
wishbone, daughter,
where your backbone
ought to be.

Clementine Paddleford

THERE'S NOTHING YOU CAN'T DO

I JUST LOVE BOSSY WOMEN... IT MEANS SOMEBODY'S PASSIONATE AND ENGAGED AND AMBITIOUS AND DOESN'T MIND LEADING.

Amy Poehler

STAY FOCUSED, GO AFTER YOUR DREAMS AND KEEP MOVING TOWARDS YOUR GOALS.

LL COOL J

IT'S NOT ABOUT
BEING THE PRETTIEST IN
THE CLASS – IT'S WHAT
YOU DO IN THE CLASS.

Victoria Beckham

Take a chance and
don't ever look back.
Never have regrets,
just lessons learned.

Kim Kardashian

GOOD THINGS COME TO THOSE WHO HUSTLE

Girl power is almost more powerful and more special than anything we are competing for.

Selena Gomez

ALWAYS REMEMBER
THAT YOU ARE
BRAVER THAN YOU
BELIEVE, STRONGER
THAN YOU SEEM
AND SMARTER
THAN YOU THINK.

A. A. Milne

IF YOU DON'T LIKE THE ROAD YOU'RE WALKING, START PAVING ANOTHER ONE.

DOLLY PARTON

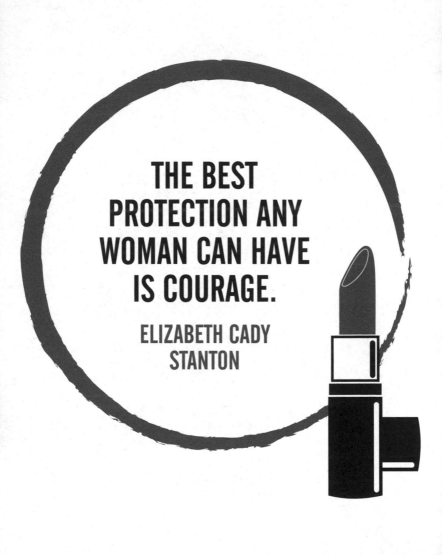

THE BEST PROTECTION ANY WOMAN CAN HAVE IS COURAGE.

ELIZABETH CADY STANTON

SLAY
ALL
DAY

I WOULD RATHER BE A REBEL THAN A SLAVE.

EMMELINE PANKHURST

THERE'S NOTHING MORE BADASS THAN BEING WHO YOU ARE.

Darren Criss

A DAME THAT KNOWS THE ROPES ISN'T LIKELY TO GET TIED UP.

MAE WEST

FIND OUT WHO YOU ARE AND BE THAT PERSON.

ELLEN DeGENERES

Namaslay

THE SLAY
IN ME
RECOGNIZES
THE SLAY
IN YOU

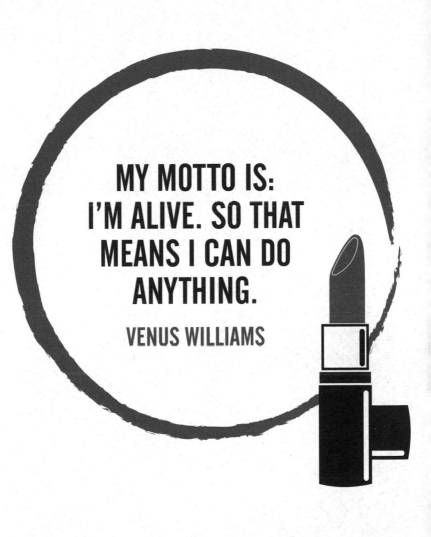

MY MOTTO IS:
I'M ALIVE. SO THAT
MEANS I CAN DO
ANYTHING.

VENUS WILLIAMS

A WINNER IS A DREAMER

WHO NEVER GIVES UP.

Nelson Mandela

If you set your mind
to something, you
can accomplish that
and then some.

Sarah Hyland

ACCEPT NOTHING BUT THE FACT THAT YOU'RE EQUAL.

Neko Case

MAKE

IT

HAPPEN!

THE QUESTION ISN'T WHO IS GOING TO LET ME; IT'S WHO IS GOING TO STOP ME.

AYN RAND

WHATEVER YOU
CAN DO, OR DREAM
YOU CAN, BEGIN IT.
BOLDNESS HAS
GENIUS, POWER
AND MAGIC IN IT.

Johann Wolfgang von Goethe

Go confidently in
the direction of your
dreams! Live the life
you've imagined.

Henry David Thoreau

MAKE EVERY MINUTE COUNT

IN THE FUTURE,
THERE WILL BE NO
FEMALE LEADERS.
THERE WILL JUST
BE LEADERS.

Sheryl Sandberg

ALL OUR DREAMS CAN COME TRUE IF WE HAVE THE COURAGE TO PURSUE THEM.

WALT DISNEY

Think like a queen.

A queen is not afraid to fail.

Failure is another stepping

stone to greatness.

Oprah Winfrey

BE THE GIRL WHO GOES FOR IT

WE NEED TO LAUGH AT THE
HATERS AND SYMPATHIZE
WITH THEM. THEY CAN
SCREAM AS LOUD AS THEY
WANT. WE CAN'T HEAR
THEM BECAUSE WE ARE
GETTING SH*T DONE.

Amy Schumer

LISTEN TO YOUR HEART ABOVE ALL OTHER VOICES.

MARTA KAGAN

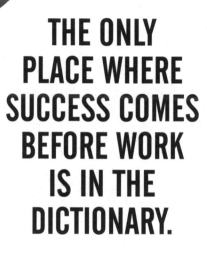

THE ONLY
PLACE WHERE
SUCCESS COMES
BEFORE WORK
IS IN THE
DICTIONARY.

VIDAL SASSOON

TAKE THE RISK OR LOSE THE CHANCE

Power means happiness;
power means hard
work and sacrifice.

Beyoncé

FORTUNE FAVORS THE BRAVE.

VIRGIL

IF YOUR DREAMS DO NOT SCARE YOU, THEY ARE NOT BIG ENOUGH.

ELLEN JOHNSON SIRLEAF

GET UP,
DRESS UP,
show up

I THINK CONFIDENCE IS THE SEXIEST THING TO HAVE.

JESSIE J

YOU CAN USE THE
SAME MOTTO FOR
EVERYTHING IN
LIFE. IF YOU PUT
THAT EFFORT IN,
YOU'LL GET WHAT
YOU WANT.

Kim Kardashian

I never underestimated
myself. And I never
saw anything wrong
with ambition.

Angela Merkel

DREAMS
DEMAND
HUSTLE

A GIRL SHOULD BE TWO THINGS: WHO AND WHAT SHE WANTS.

COCO CHANEL

YOU HAVE WHAT
IT TAKES TO BE
A VICTORIOUS,
INDEPENDENT,
FEARLESS WOMAN.

Tyra Banks

IT ALWAYS SEEMS IMPOSSIBLE UNTIL IT'S DONE.

NELSON MANDELA

TURN A SETBACK INTO A COMEBACK

IF YOU KNOW
YOU'RE GREAT AT
WHAT YOU DO,
DON'T EVER BE
ASHAMED TO ASK
FOR THE TOP DOLLAR
IN YOUR FIELD.

Nicki Minaj

I'M TOUGH, I'M AMBITIOUS,
AND I KNOW EXACTLY
WHAT I WANT.

Madonna

I'd rather regret the things I've done than regret the things I haven't done.

Lucille Ball

INHALE
CONFIDENCE;
EXHALE
DOUBT

FOREVER IS COMPOSED OF NOWS.

EMILY DICKINSON

AND THOUGH
SHE BE BUT
LITTLE, SHE
IS FIERCE.

WILLIAM
SHAKESPEARE

The most effective way
to do it, is to do it.

Amelia Earhart

LIFE IS TOUGH, BUT
so are you

A WISE GIRL KNOWS HER LIMITS BUT A SMART GIRL KNOWS SHE HAS NONE.

MARILYN MONROE

BE SO GOOD THEY CAN'T IGNORE YOU.

STEVE MARTIN

Don't count the days,
make the days count.

Muhammad Ali

REAL QUEENS FIX EACH OTHER'S CROWNS

IF YOU HELP SOMEONE ELSE SUCCEED, YOU TOO SHALL SUCCEED. I RISE WHEN OTHERS RISE.

Gina Rodriguez

YOU'VE GOT TO GET UP
EVERY MORNING WITH
DETERMINATION IF YOU'RE
GOING TO GO TO BED
WITH SATISFACTION.

George Lorimer

I would rather die of passion
than of boredom.

Émile Zola

NOTHING CAN DIM THE LIGHT WHICH SHINES FROM WITHIN.

MAYA ANGELOU

ALWAYS
HAVE CLASS
BUT ALWAYS
KICK ASS

I FINALLY GOT
MY ANSWER TO
THAT QUESTION:
WHO DO YOU
THINK YOU ARE?
I AM WHOEVER
I SAY I AM.

America Ferrera

THE SECRET OF GETTING AHEAD IS GETTING STARTED.

MARK TWAIN

Just try new things.
Don't be afraid. Step
out of your comfort
zones and soar.

Michelle Obama

NOBODY CAN HOLD YOU BACK

FEET, WHAT
DO I NEED
YOU FOR IF
I HAVE WINGS
TO FLY?

FRIDA KAHLO

IF YOU WANT SOMETHING, GO GET IT. PERIOD.

WILL SMITH

IF YOU REST,
YOU RUST.

HELEN HAYES

MISTAKES
ARE PROOF
THAT YOU
ARE TRYING

YOU NEED TO
FIND THE POWER
WITHIN TO MAKE
THINGS HAPPEN
FOR YOURSELF.
WHEN YOU REALIZE
THIS, YOU ARE
UNSTOPPABLE.

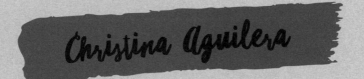

Christina Aguilera

DON'T BE AFRAID TO SPEAK UP FOR YOURSELF. KEEP FIGHTING FOR YOUR DREAMS!

GABBY DOUGLAS

YOU CAN, YOU SHOULD,
AND IF YOU'RE BRAVE
ENOUGH TO START,
YOU WILL.

Stephen King

YOU ONLY LIVE ONCE SO YOU MIGHT AS WELL

be a badass

I figure, if a girl wants to be a legend, she should just go ahead and be one.

Calamity Jane

BE THE GIRL WITH GRIT AND GRACE

I LOVE TO SEE A
YOUNG GIRL GO
OUT AND GRAB
THE WORLD BY
THE LAPELS.

MAYA ANGELOU

IF YOUR SHIP DOESN'T COME IN, SWIM OUT TO IT.

JONATHAN WINTERS

Change your life today. Don't gamble on the future, act now, without delay.

simone de Beauvoir

GRIND 'TIL YOU OWN IT

A STRONG WOMAN LOOKS A CHALLENGE DEAD IN THE EYE AND GIVES IT A WINK.

GINA CAREY

SHOOT FOR THE MOON.
EVEN IF YOU MISS, YOU'LL
LAND AMONG THE STARS.

Les Brown

REALLY TRY TO FOLLOW WHAT IT IS THAT YOU WANT TO DO AND WHAT YOUR HEART IS TELLING YOU TO DO.

Jennifer Aniston

FALL SEVEN
TIMES.
STAND
UP EIGHT.

JAPANESE PROVERB

IF YOU
STUMBLE,
MAKE IT PART
OF YOUR
DANCE

You can do anything
you set your mind to.

Benjamin Franklin

LUCK IS A DIVIDEND OF SWEAT. THE MORE YOU SWEAT, THE LUCKIER YOU GET.

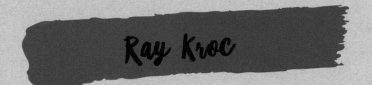

Ray Kroc

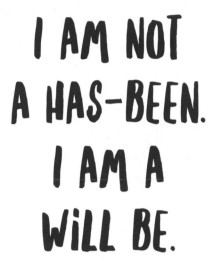

I AM NOT
A HAS-BEEN.
I AM A
WILL BE.

LAUREN BACALL

IF YOU CAN BELIEVE IN SOMETHING GREAT, THEN YOU CAN ACHIEVE SOMETHING GREAT.

KATY PERRY

TURN CAN'TS INTO CANS AND DREAMS INTO PLANS

I BELIEVE AMBITION IS NOT A DIRTY WORD. IT'S JUST BELIEVING IN YOURSELF AND YOUR ABILITIES.

Reese Witherspoon

OUR GREATEST GLORY IS NOT IN NEVER FALLING, BUT IN RISING EVERY TIME WE FALL.

CONFUCIUS

Sometimes the smallest step in the right direction ends up being the biggest step of your life.

Emma Stone

BE THE GIRL WITH GOALS

THE ROAD TO SUCCESS IS ALWAYS UNDER CONSTRUCTION.

LILY TOMLIN

WORK HARD IN SILENCE. LET YOUR SUCCESS BE THE NOISE.

FRANK OCEAN

THERE'S NO BETTER MAKE-UP THAN SELF-CONFIDENCE.

SHAKIRA

I THINK THAT NOT BEING PERFECT HAS GIVEN ME THE FREEDOM TO KEEP GETTING BETTER.

Gigi Hadid

TODAY IS A
GOOD DAY TO
slay

THERE IS NO CHANCE, NO DESTINY, NO FATE, THAT CAN CIRCUMVENT OR HINDER OR CONTROL THE FIRM RESOLVE OF A DETERMINED SOUL.

Ella Wheeler Wilcox

BE
YOURSELF.
NO ONE
ELSE CAN.

HELENA BONHAM
CARTER

THERE IS NO LIMIT TO WHAT WE, AS WOMEN, CAN ACCOMPLISH.

MICHELLE OBAMA

BE BRAVE,
BE BOLD,
BE FREE.

ANGELINA JOLIE

If you're interested in finding out more about our books, find us on Facebook at **Summersdale Publishers** and follow us on Twitter at **@Summersdale**.

www.summersdale.com

#SLAY